That Said

That Said

New and Selected Poems

ROBERT SCHREUR

Syllabic Press

BALTIMORE, MARYLAND

ISBN-13: 978-0692994764

Syllabic
■Press

200 E. Joppa Road, Suite L-101
Towson, MD 21286
syllabicpress@gmail.com

Library of Congress Control Number: 2017919134
Syllabic Press, Towson, MD

Cover photo: Robert Schreur

Contents

from INTRODUCTION TO MICROECONOMICS

from THE COMMUTE

from THE MOON ON THE STAIRS:
   A BOOK OF CHILDREN'S VERSE

from OF LATE

from NOTHING MUCH

from RESULTS

from AT THE LEAST

from POEMS AND PROBLEMS

from A KNIFE IN MEN'S EYES *and uncollected poems*

That Said

New Poems

My Happiness

after Nietzsche

Seeking was too tiring
so I learned how to find.
The wind went against me
so I went with the wind.

My Complaint

after Hoccleve

After the sheaves were tied in
and the brown season began
robbing the trees of the leaves
that once were a lusty green
but now were dull yellowness
and thrown down flat underfoot,
a change sank to my heart's root

refreshing my memory
that nothing here is stable,
nothing true but variance,
no matter how well begun
nothing lasts, all is foregone,
all gets driven and thrust down
to the selfsame conclusion

that no one can circumvent,
not with wealth or force or joy,
so that by late November
I was laid up, bedridden
with my thoughts and lack of sleep
and this vexing malady
had all but burned my eyes dry

and I watched as the sickness
scourged and darkened the favors
that once had poured down on me,
as though a black rain had struck
and left me drowning, awash
in loss, a pitiful sight,
destitute, without delight,

my heart so bloated with grief,
my brain so throbbing and gorged,
I had to find a way out,
no way could I keep it in
till I was old and grey—so
I looked back at what came first
and felt something inside burst.

My Poems

after Mallarmé

Though they sometimes do evoke
a certain sort of order
they're more like watching one smoke
ring fade into another

like when you have a cigar
lit and drawing perfectly
and you see the ashes are
what lips soon enough will be—

better to stifle the cough
stuck at the back of your throat
than admit there's no payoff
in spouting truths (quote-unquote)—

there's no need to try and cure
what pleasures like these obscure.

My Shadow

I concede
the sun's strength
so far off
but I swear
my shadow
is the smoke
from a fire
far inside,
and there's proof:

at night when
I'm enflamed
and the sun
is nowhere
to be seen
then shadows
fill my room
and black soot
smothers me.

Among Friends

after Nietzsche

It's good to be quiet together
but to laugh together's better yet,
beneath the silky sheets of the skies,
leaning backs against moss and birch trees,
having a tremendous time of it,
showing our white teeth to each other...

At Whitman's Tomb

... look for me under your boot-soles

Curiously, to use a favorite Whitman word, there actually was a boot. It was half-buried in mud, partway up the small hill the tomb was dug into. (When Whitman came to inspect the tomb he climbed this hill to take a leak.) Now late spring rains had made the ground the same soggy black as the greasy boot. Near it were a car headlamp half full of brown water, some broken bottles, all the usual urban refuse. It seemed morbid or silly to reflect that Whitman actually was to be found under this boot, but he had wanted to be taken literally, not to mention prophetically.

Also curious, but more disturbing, was the oily black carcass of a goose rotting on the gravel path that led to the gated vault. Flocks of self-important geese were patrolling the cemetery, but this one looked cooked and tossed away. Who knew what had happened to it or how long it had been there. Maybe it had died in November. That would make for a nice consonance with the Old German word for November, *Gänsemonat*, meaning "goose-month." But then why are geese also identified with summer, as in the word *gossamer*, "goose-summer"? Maybe goose-summer is the equivalent of our Indian summer, when geese fly south and gossamer cobwebs drift through the autumn air.

Anyway, winter had not treated the bird well. Maybe soon a groundskeeper would clean it up along with the notes and trinkets others had left in front of the tomb. These could be called "keepsakes," or more accurately "leave-behind-sakes." No one would call them litter in this context, but a strong wind could easily blow some into the nearby pond, where they would become trash for the geese to peck through.

Still, there really was no virtue in having brought nothing to lay at the grave or throw to the birds. Just visiting there, just bringing one's thoughts, contributed to the debris, what Whitman had called "chaff" and "scum" and, in a dark mood, "the slag and hideous rot." All this was disheartening.

> To call on
> the interred
> half bent on
> entering
>
> in under
> a lintel
> and into
> a center
>
> thereby by
> bodily
> being there
> intending
>
> to reverse
> or at worst
> to stem the
> dispersal

though one's own
ash would soon
be strewn as
the trash was

was to lend
breadcrumbs fit
for geese to
a dead one.

The car tires crackled on the crumbling macadam path that led back into Camden. The geese resentfully scuffled aside, but they seemed certain to stay through the summer. There was little sense of the seasonal pulse and purpose Whitman once recorded in a sixty-six syllable line.

> *The migrating flock of wild geese alighting in autumn to*
> *refresh themselves, the body of the flock feed, the sentinels*
> *out-side move around with erect heads watching, and are*
> *from time to time reliev'd by other sentinels—and I feed-*
> *ing and taking turns with the rest.*

The goal now was to leave behind the smallest footprint possible.

H.D.'s Grave

Snow swept the gravestone,
seashells others left,
and some ice-swollen
white, little flowers—
Star of Bethlehem.

Corfu, Luxor, Crete.
None traveled farther
to return to rest
nearer her birthplace,
a long astral arc.

One loves in her verse
"a self-possession
forever in fear
of losing itself"—
in fear, not despair—

as well as the *strained
inappropriate
allusions*, knowing
how the *awareness
leaves us defenseless,*

standing there adrift
in the wind's eddies,
till a drift of snow
slides from a branch—then
silence more intense.

Agenda

In Endymion, I leaped headlong into the Sea
—*Keats*

It's heartrending
though endearing
how we intend
to descend to
stupendous depths
only to end
up upended
off the deep end.

We so depend
on splendid forms
to suspend us
we pretend they
must portend some
rendezvous to
surrender to
or apprehend.

Grievances

Not to gainsay
our gains or say
that all we gain
is gained again
after it's gone

or take with grains
of salt each grace
or for granted
our garnerings
are ill-gotten

still in the grand
scheme we find ground
granules of loss
like grit that grates
against the grain

and gainful though
the gettings be
how ungainly
these graspings for
what's still ungleaned.

Worthwhile

1

Words worth
their weight
were worth
the wait

no worse
for where
they'd worn
away

for when
they weighed
our worth
their wealth

outweighed
our worst.

2

At worst
their worth
withstood
our wiles

and while
our work
all went
to waste

wages
which we
withdrew
with words

were worth
our while.

What Matters

As a matter of
fact matters of fact
matter no matter
what is the matter.

In fact the fact of
the matter is the
fact of matter is
what is the matter.

To make matters worse
it's just a matter
of time till matter
makes time not matter,

till we take matters
in our own hands and
find matter is the
end of the matter.

Elevator Story

Here's what happened.
The doors opened
and the riders
bid me riddance.
So I told them
it comes down to
not what happens
but whom it will
have happened to
and wherever
they were going
down to I was
going down too
and whatever
took us down would
have already
taken its toll
not that we are
good for it but
that we're done for
ready or not.
I took the stares
and took the stairs.

Embedded

After I dig
out from under
each night's slag heap
and shake the shale
from my raw hands

I stare back down
the narrow shaft
hoping to catch
gleams of some dream
I'd not unearthed.

Quarry

Are the heaps
I amass
dross I sluice
some flakes from

or hoardings
of some past
from which slight
glitters come?

Trouble the Water

Though our sleep
is troubled
all day long
our troubles
long for sleep

till day's end
they descend
to the murk
and turmoil
of our dreams

as spilt oil
slicks the waves
and finally
sinks sicken-
ing the deep.

For the Most Part

Often after
a feather falls
more stillnesses,
more hush follow.

Hardly ever drop
wing, beak, talon,
rarely falcon,
seldom swallow.

Reverie

Whether like bees
we will hover
over our graves
or like clover
cover over
the depths death braves,

other lovers
will uncover
if not aver
secrets we have
hid forever
deep in our days.

Halves

Having waited
without having
till halfway done

to have to wait
for what's now had
is half the fun.

The Present

I loved
now once
for what
would be

but love
now now
for what
once was.

Soundings

In shallows
we founder.

Profounder
we flounder.

Knickknack

No knock
on you
nor to
nitpick
but in
my neck
of the
woods we
nip the
buds in
the nick
of time.

Pietà

Avert your eyes
from what those hands
held only twice,
in infancy
and now again
with all withheld.

Your as of yet
unbroken heart
is now beheld
by eyes whose grief
was never meant
to be dispelled.

Our Portion

Within some set
parameters
we may merit
the punishments
the world metes out

yet its measures
are so extreme
we must suppose
we too surpass
all proportion.

Beloved

Before when I'd
made a beeline
to your beehive

I half-believed
I behaved on
my own behalf

but what befell
belies the thought
and it behooves

me now bereft
to behold how
beholden I've

become, beckoned
into the blue
at your behest.

News to Me

With you came something new,
new sorrow, new to me.

I thought I knew sorrow
thoroughly before you.

I thought I knew sorrow
through and through. Before you

I thought sorrow could be
known through. But now I know

sorrow when known through you
is sorrow known anew.

New sorrow came with you
and now tomorrow you

will renew the sorrow
you came with, the sorrow

you're known for, as though you
knew only new sorrow

would make you known to me,
would make you new to me.

Onto Me

I'd say my sighs
were for her eyes
but she'd surmise
they're for her thighs.

Middle-aged

No longer
a not yet.

Not yet a
no longer.

That Said

So much was said so as to say no more.
As such such as was said was said no more.
So what was said was to be said no more.
And what was said to be was said no more.
Such that what was was said to be no more.

No more was what was said last said to last.
To say so was what was to be said last.
To say no more was to say so at last.
And what was said was so to say said last.
That said so much more was to last no more.

For the Clouds

Though they frequent
the firmament
they are first and
foremost terra
firma's frailest
ephemera,
films frothing the
formidable
mountains, flimsy,
forgettable,
their features mere
metaphors for
fur, for firs, ferns,
feathers, formless
otherwise, failed
effronteries,
formulae for
fragility,
briefest forests
of forms foregone,
and but for their
aforementioned
frequency no
forbearance, no
forgiveness should
be afforded

them, their farfetched
phosphorescence
their own affair,
were their forte
not to affirm
one's own forays
at forever.

from INTRODUCTION TO MICROECONOMICS
(1996)

Money money money
Water water water
            —*Theodore Roethke*

Work

The work bees do is not our work.
Busy, wayward, lascivious,
names we give to call them back.
Still they are not ours.

Call it greatness, the delay
we formulate and inform. Marx did.
Greatness keeps me up at night,
busy, wayward, lascivious.

Sunrise, Sunset

Pink at night and no sailor in sight.
When you figure maxims out
they don't apply, or not anymore.
You even wonder where the sailors were.

Like when your mother tells you
to floss your teeth and you've just lost
your girl and for once you sleep till morning,
the sky pink and your gums bleeding.

Opening Theory

After you bring the king's pawn
forward, that should about do it.
Granted, more moves may be required,
each one intricate, treacherous, foolhardy,

bold, forced, or wooden.
But in the end each only makes good
what was definitively asserted
in your first, small gesture.

Supply and Demand

The movement that persists
when the movement passes
like ants come out again
after the hour's rain

and the light above the elm
like milk around your tongue
ask less of us than you think.
You ask enough to make up for them.

Men at Work

By this late date we will have figured
our desires out, how they make
the world they do, how
they put the questions on the plate.

The best of us will be ashamed
to have become so obvious.
Everything they said was true.
Penises come and go. The work remains.

The Editors

This sentence is left incomplete.
The handwriting here is illegible.
At this point in the manuscript
there is a diagram, three short lines

meet at a point. How it relates
to the paragraph is unclear to us.
In the margin of the page
is a drawing of a human face.

Schooldays

All the little desks and the large one
up front, hooks for hats and coats,
pencils lost on the playground,
a dusty eraser, colored paper,

bells, the musky boredom
of small hands and feet. Hands
pledged across hearts. Feet under desks.
My hand raised to answer.

Poem

And that's just it, each one
pretends to know what you're thinking,
when, if you think about it,
that's not it at all.

It's a whole nother problem.
You can't even be sure they give
the thoughts you have to think.
Nobody knows the trouble you've seen.

Matthew 6:31-34

We're worriers. What's to eat?
Where're the drinks? What should I wear?
Of course, that's not really what we want.
Say it, we want the kingdom of God,

that purity. The other stuff keeps coming,
the worry it might stop tomorrow.
But we know today's what's worrying.
Today's sufficient for the evil hereof.

Fragment

for the same reason in likeness

little else but a naked intent

the meekness, the substance
whoso might get these clear

and be it evil, a passing comfort

hastily the ears of the hearers
without departing
to other comforts and sounds

Questions for Review

What was set upon a golden bough?
Is money a kind of poetry?
Who glittered when he walked?
Whose woods were they? What was the dream

in the peasant's bent shoulders?
Why was the figure 5 in gold?
Do you know nothing? Do you see nothing?
Do you too dislike it? Explain.

Notes

It is not what you say.
It is not what you think.
It is not what you do.
It is not what you wear.

It is not what you eat.
It is not where you've been.
It is not who you are.
It is not what you've done.

Biography

Saint Augustine had God explain
why his ears itched,
why he had stolen the pears.
God is there to give biography,

as if we need an excuse. We do.
My name is Robert Schreur.
Nothing will explain
what has happened to me.

from THE COMMUTE
(1998)

Surely, the tide comes in twice a day.
                    —*Charles Reznikoff*

The Interstate

Already the trees bleed their briefest colors.
Leaves spot the once-dead wood.
On my drive, maples flaunt their damask
buds and dogwoods gaudy blooms. Even
the jerks, who switch lanes without looking
for me in their blind spot, see them.

Already it's too late for the poem I wanted
to write, about how the sweet air
kissed my eyes as they looked out over
the still-bare bark, about how
the sun's lingering days spread sap
up my body's long capillary wicks
and the world stayed ignorant of my joy.

Again I'm taught to share the interstate.

The Ditch

Off to my right I saw a ditch, set back
from the road and rimmed by tall weeds, with weeds
within and matted grass and dirt. The earth
was puckered there like a still-warm pillow.
My lungs sighed, and my head, glacier-like,
thought to rest like Wordsworth, to weep like Rossetti.

My eyes, too, gave way, leaving my hands
and the hands of other drivers to see me through.

Which they did, and do each time I risk
my neck to check out those I pass, avid
to size up how they look and what they're driving,
to make out the fleeting lines and lost faces,
as though my heart forever ached to know
what it can want and still pass by.

The New Building

The excavating continues below my office.
I look down on shovels, backhoes, mixers,
the things with which the mind of boyhood thinks.
The pit they've sunk for counterweight has deepened
into gold, then copper earth. The boys'
minds have delved down deep, coming
up with this, erecting on paper and soon
in air models of the fathers' world.

Corporate America has dug another hole.
I see it now: the new building's arrogant,
complacent lines will block my view of older
ones. I could care less. Put it up.
My profound indifference has at last become
the very emblem of my soul's perfection.

Relief

I appease the present urge to write by looking
to notes I wrote awhile ago, then
tentative and partial but now englobed
in the dim aura of forgotten knowledge.

Once there, the work of reclamation serves
the muse in her absence or postulates a muse
where none was before. Don't ask. I've
never met her. I wouldn't know what to say.

But after that poem is done, another one
often—I almost said always—comes to me,
not better, but a relief, like a first date
after the marriage has withered like dusk and
your voice returns in a stranger's bed like dawn,
like the voice the poem has given you to write.

Where Each Leads

I send you my thoughts, still thinking
you can use them when I cannot.

When I began to write, the sun shone
on my lap. Now it shines at my side. I've had
a dozen thoughts, none of which I've followed
out, having rejected where each leads.

I have a friend who believes some grad
student will collect her papers and submit to the truth
of her thoughts. She writes him everyday
and keeps back things he shouldn't know.

I tell her to give it up. Write it all
down. No one will read it. But maybe she's right.
Fame is had to be shared. Well, not mine.
Mine I've buried with all I've hid in the earth.

What? Where?

How soon I've forgotten my day. It's after six.
I'm passing some trees. If I could see more clearly
this dog-eared night might unfold into
an image of the world, its laws and limits
repeated in the compacts of self-interest.

The cars inside the lines. The pine stems
assembled against the fading sky. The sky
itself officed with presences, dark
or darkening... I cannot sustain the thought.
My days and nights divulge almost nothing.

Is it this inarticulateness, this way
the world gives way without giving itself
away, that I would praise, remark to praise?

No. My interests lie elsewhere. I don't know where.

Body of Knowledge

after Verlaine

Again it comes to me, how dejected the body
is. How tired. It makes me want to cry.

The body buried in the blackness of sleep,
its hands like dead animals pressed down:
as, shivering toward tomorrow's fever
and itching at the dried sweat of today,
a bird hunkers under the rain gutter.

My foot is throbbing from the punishing highway.
My chest feels like a fist has punched it twice.
My mouth tastes blood from three open sores.
My skin trembles near the TV screen.
And my eyes? My eyes are growing brilliant from
seeing the point of all this looking away.

Pathetic body, so hopeless and so hurt.

Redoubtable

Coaxed from chaos, chided out of childhood,
I wound my way, weary, restless, wide-eyed,
staring toward some stream's shady source,
and turned away, stricken by time's thick tinctures.
Memories of maples and milkweed grew more obscure,
earth's intricate intensity, opaque.

I collected color, accumulated clutter.
My head held hubbubs of hermetic litter,
and bore it no better when, bored, urbane, brutal,
I laid waste to what little I loved, leveled it all,
only to find in fragments of feeling figments
remembered, which scarred like rain the rain-swollen rivers.

Yet always the amateur, eager for ending,
I broke with belief, abetting the days, abiding.

Autumn, Giving In

I look at the trees I pass, almost aghast:
the world in dying becomes yet more distinct.
I'd gotten used to the steady blur of green,
to say "trees" and "leaves" and mean the scene I saw.

I'd add to these "the ground," "the sky," and there
would be the world. I could easily imagine
it was a dream, a painted screen my eyes
could not see past, enclosing my driven heart.

Bored and blank, my stare would wash away
unconscionable details everywhere I'd look—
the particulars not only of her face,
but of each stone, each cloud, each greeny leaf.

Now all these separate colors. These reds! These yellows!
My God! is this the only world there is?

After Hours

You say I talk in my sleep. Last night you talked
in yours. "Stop," you said. And then, "stay here."
I answered with, "where?" which I know was dumb, but I
was tired and didn't know what else to say.

I wonder if we ever talk together
in our sleep, your words answering mine without
our effort, making sense without our knowing,
as computers do our banking after hours.

The idea sends a thrill along my spine
that we should be connected so, beyond
our waking selves, should be linked someway
and talk as lovers talk who have nothing to say.

And isn't that how it always is? Our bodies
speak. I do not know what I am saying.

The Commute

I probably should've listened to tapes. I might
've learned to fathom Bird or Bach, or taught
myself Chinese or French. I should've used
the time behind the wheel, the hours spent.

Going there and coming back, along
for the ride, I wonder what, if anything,
the soul acquires, what knowledge it puts on.
What can it learn from anything I've done?

I humor myself it's not so bad I don't
know other languages: I hardly know
my own. It's hard to hear the songs I can't
forget. Wherever I go, it seems, I'm no-
where nearer to whatever it is I want.
Circling back, with nothing more to show.

Calisthenic

Of all I have read I have absorbed
almost nothing. What I retain
becomes more fat than muscle.

I write these poems to burn off the fat.

Late November

Leaves have fallen everywhere.

This one fell
in my open book.

The Wet Wood

whistles in the fire.
It does not stop to take a breath.

Fruit

Lately the pleasure of eating fruit has been
the thought I'm eating a tree.

Down by the River

So Achilles wouldn't drown,
his mother held him by the heel.

Mine held me by the hand
to keep my head from going under.

Interlude

Where two buildings abut,
brown leaves circle about.

A sheet of paper circles with them.

from THE MOON ON THE STAIRS:
A BOOK OF CHILDREN'S VERSE
(1999)

What? Where?

There's a laugh
In the grass.
I don't know whose it is.

There's a song
Near there stream.
I don't know who is singing.

There's gold
In my hair.
Who could have put it there?

There are letters
In the tree,
An *A*, a *B*, a *C*.

There's smiling
In the wind.
But who knows where or when.

There's a spark
In the dark,
And then it's gone again.

Things Grandma Said

Once she walked a little way
      And I ran on ahead.
"A thimble full of yesterday,"
      Is what she said.
          —Silver thimble.

Once she waited by the river
      As clouds sped overhead.
"Not a pin, not even a sliver,"
      Is what she said.
          —Tiny pin.

I asked her if she liked the spring
      Or autumn best instead.
"Birds in nests, birds on the wing,"
      Is what she said.
          —Busy birds.

I asked her why she slept in chairs
      And not her double bed.
"Moonlight stepping down the stairs,"
      Is what she said.
          —Careful moon.

I watched her fingers turning pages
In the book she read.
"Kings and queens and clowns on stages,"
Is what she said.
—Old, old play.

Two Books

The *smallest* book I ever saw
Was devoted to the law.
Everything you should not do
(And if you did, what would happen to you)
Was on *one* page, about so wide,
And it was blank on the other side.
All the law you needed to know
Was just one word. The word was *no*.

The *biggest* book I ever read
Was entirely inside my head.
Everything I wanted to do
(Everything you could do, too)
Was written out a *million* times
On every page in perfect rhymes.
Describing all this wishfulness
Was just one word—*yes, yes, yes, yes*...

Clouds

On summer days with hours to gaze
It used to be that folks would see
Shapes of things like garden swings
And ducks and brooms and coffee spoons
In the lazy crowds of drifting clouds.
Lincoln's face and grandma's lace
Would be up there, a rocking chair,
A sweetheart's lips, tall sailing ships.

So yesterday on my way
Out to the car, which wasn't far,
I stopped and took a hurried look
And thought I saw: Bugs Bunny's paw!
A skateboard ramp, a lava lamp!
A plastic Slinky, a half-eaten Twinkie!
I rode to the mall, scratching my skull.
Something has changed. Are the clouds deranged?

Five Contrasts

1

Eyes have blinds
To hide what they are.
Ears are doors
Forever ajar.

2

We hold our heads high in the air,
Our arms and legs are pointed down.
Trees reach their limbs up to the sky
And root their brains down in the ground.

3

Until they're too short,
Pencils scribble along.
Eraser's can't write,
But they never are wrong.

4

Computers get faster
Each new model year.
Books stay as slow
As the day they appear.

Clouds cloud.
Mirrors mirror.

Too Many Clothes

Needless needles,
Pointless pins:
A yard of cloth
And trouble begins.

Nimble thimbles,
Sprocketed spools:
A thousand tailors
On a thousand stools.

Don't get them started!
Don't let them sit!
Once they are stitching
You can't make them quit.

I needed one shirt,
The tailor made two.
Most make too many,
So few sew too few.

Early Blooms

It's early spring, the earth is cold,
     The air is cold above.
When we take our morning walk
     I put on boots and gloves.

No one is out, except the flowers
     Huddled in trees along our street.
It's early spring, the ground's too cold
     For their tender feet.

Infant Thoughts

Both eyes open
And in pours light.

Hungry cries
Bring milk at night.

I'm lifted up
And moved around.

My limbs bend
Without a sound.

Breath flows in
And floats away.

Moon-smells at night,
Sun-smells by day.

This and That

Thunder dark
And lightning bright.
Dogs that bark
And dogs that bite.

Stairways up
And stairways down.
A half-full cup,
A turned-over frown.

The sun by day
And stars by night.
Doors that sway
And doors shut tight.

The brilliant rose,
The hidden thorn.
What comes and goes,
What dies and is born.

Joys that laugh
And joys that cry.
You know half
When you ask why.

To and Fro

Above a stream the boulder moon
Rises now but will sink soon.

In my hand a moonlit rock.
I hold it then I throw it back.

Tonight I'll search a silver stream.
Tomorrow I'll know it was a dream.

Here and there and to and fro,
Moon and rocks and people go.

from OF LATE
(2000)

Birdcall

From early this morning,
the song and dance of birds—
he looks, but does not see,
listens, doesn't hear.

They quote from Isaiah,
but if it's laughter or lament or neither,
I do not know.

Like Jacob

I too wrestled an angel.
In fact, it may have been God.

I still get pains in my hip
where the pale hand
perturbed at my importunity
struck.

But I kept my name.

Geology

Near the summit
rocks ducked beneath the wind.
The fields were shifting tiles.

What with the whirling sun
and weeds twisting like horses,
you'd have thought the gospel would come true,
that my silence would make the rocks cry out.

They would not have been rocks
were they not prepared to wait
a billion years.

Hydrology

I was alone and wanting words to come—
as if they were rain and would fill
the little hole I dug for them.

Better, I thought, to scoop a pit in the shore
and wait as from underneath the water comes
and swells the sand in the pit
until it is no more.

Bright Lights, Big City

Like a small-town boy
entering New York,
I believed in one God,
if that,
and found myself before

echelons.

Three Sentences

after Angelus Silesius

I love not knowing,
which is why I love.

.

Too bad we're not like birds
whose songs attract them to each other.

.

Deep calls to deep, but which
is buried deeper, God or I?

The Net

I want to tell my love
but my words are fish—
a seine keeps them
from going downstream,
the smallest ones cannot get through.

How would you know
but for the water rushing
rushing through the net?

After Sappho

I have a son
better than
a small well-printed book.

I wouldn't trade
the library at Alexandria
and all its knowledge
for him.

Divine Comedy

When heaven and earth were opened to me,
I was not given an epic to write.

I alone can read the thousand cantos
hidden away in one of my lines.

To _____

I have lived with your poems for twenty years.
I will not presume to speak.

In twenty more I may be able to say
what already I feel.

Sandstone

The writing I have done
has been written on sand.

I wait for those who have done otherwise
to cast the first stone.

Sticktoitiveness

I began, knowing it was a mistake.

Now it would be a mistake to stop.

After Bashō

Away from Baltimore
I see an oriole
and know I am away.

Rage

Because it sounds so angry
I keep checking if the bee
is trapped inside the screen.

No, it's trapped outside.

Had I Not Known

the airport was nearby
I would have thought a star
had come inside
this dome of clouds.

Acoustics

Is that muted roar
a bumblebee near the door
or a truck an acre away?

Consolation

At first I was angry—
a mouse had nibbled
my favorite book.

It's alright, I said.
I have done no more.

Half Measures

Not the river,
not the surging known and bright,
but the stream
half-frozen in December.

Not the vision,
not the image open to sight,
but the dream
in the morning half-remembered.

At the Printshop

for my father

Before the printed sheet,
before the first impression,
before the chuckling gears
and the roller's hum,

a knife must spread the ink,
thicker than blood.

The Origin of Chess

a legend from India

To tell her the unspeakable news
the messenger made up a game
and showed her how the pieces moved
like parts of speech, so that
in time she would win and say
"checkmate" and he could reply
(though here the etymology is false)
"yes, the king your son is dead."

Just Now

It was only yesterday
I made these nervous things.
More than likely tomorrow
will bring me more of them.

But a light breeze today
has brushed them away.

Song

The leaf that was stranded
at the edge of the stream,
gripped by rocks and stems,
is loosed to the current again.

I would thank whatever gods may be,
the strict and gentle gods of poetry.

from NOTHING MUCH
(2002)

I bow to all
my body knows,

head and shoulders,
knees and toes.

When I kiss
my soul comes
to my lips,
at a loss
how to cross
this small abyss.

Seesaw

I know
I did
not see
what now
I know
I saw.

Not given
a vision
of things
above
I saw
a woman
made happy
in love.

Trifle

If it fits
infinity
fits in it.

Narrowed
down not
to what
I saw
but to
what what
I saw
showed.

As much
as I
wanted much
much less
even least
was best.

A sunlit shelf
for two small pots
to hold what is
and what is not.

Though I hunger
for the first
it is the other
slakes my thirst.

The snow is off
the garden wall
on which one summer
my son would crawl.

Older he told me
what poetry is.
"It doesn't seem true
but it is."

from RESULTS
(2003)

Might many
do what
one had
not or
was one
enough if
not forgot?

Dialogue

Like part
to whole,
said heart
to soul.

Wholly
apart,
said soul
to heart.

Prayer

Forgive us this day
our daily bread,
we whose place
is set instead.

It got
so what
I thought
about
was what
I thought
thought was
about.

I found
out what
I found
out I
could do
without.

Memento mori

I lull
in one
cupped hand
my skull,
trying
comforts
I'll not
recall.

Stars drown
in dawn skies
to resurface
in dark eyes.

The knots I knew
were simple ones
for shoestrings and ribbons.

Over under through—
no good on galleons
but perfect for you.

All Night

Wind whined,
let me in.

Already are,
sighed mind.

With each step
down the steep
drop stones drop
deeper yet.

Hand and foot,
root and branch—
I my own
avalanche.

Bottle broken
in the brown bag
the drunkard dropped—

love too discards,
the soul in shards,
the body slumped.

Who wrote these lines
beneath my eyes,
so careful and neat?

If age, will he
likewise be
their exegete?

I was told to
show results.
I thought they said,
sow your faults.

Whatever. My way
is fits and halts,
long pauses, then
somersaults.

from AT THE LEAST
(2005)

Inverse

The one
before
means all
the more
the less
one knows
what this
one's for.

Voicing

To the wind
are sounds sand
in the wound
or like waves
to the shore
are they salves?

Drift

What took
me years
to see
now takes
the years
from me.

The Opening

I chose doors
that opened
to roses

and not roads
that rose to
the open.

A Day

A dew.
Ado.
Adieu.

Work Song

Each night I lose
the thread to clues
I search all day
for in the fray.

Relic

On the sill
the circle
where the vase
of roses
stood until
what little
I had had
had faded.

The Empty Hand

All I ask
is a task
to do, then
to know when.

Condensation

Out loud
words cloud.

Put down
they drown.

Words

Each I
eschew
is one
too few.

Notwithstanding

Better
all told
that I
withhold
what I behold
than tell
as I
am told.

Dream Song

2 a.m. A bird.
I knew for certain
it sang for my sake.

But did it intend
to put me to sleep
or sing me awake?

Nothing Doing

Nothing to do it to,
nothing to do to it.

Nothing to do it with,
nothing to do with it.

Nothing to do it for,
nothing to do for it.

With nothing else to do,
to do it for nothing.

No Telling

Of all that lets me be
I cannot tell apart
occurrences that dart
obliquely off, from those
that fasten more deeply
in than thought ever goes.

Threshing

Not my words,
which are chaff,
but their gist
is the grist
for your mill.

Winnow me,
world, till just
what I mean
will remain
to be said.

The Retort

I leave behind
fullness of world
for empty self
only to fill
with self the world
I leave to find.

Noon

In the ruins
under the glare
I walk head down
not in despair
but to find coins
good everywhere.

All in All

For all I
long for all
I lack all
I look for
is longing
looking back.

Portrait

I turn away
to draw the shape
of having been

and look again
to see the look
of being seen.

Ravishment

Proximity
to simplest fact
brings intellect
to ecstasy.

Acolyte

What brilliant flames
so blinded me
that these dark forms
are all I see?

His	Hers
On the mind,	Makeup,
on the make,	make out,
on the mark,	make up,
on the mend.	make do.

Bloomsday

Nothing in mind
as I went out,
same old houses,
familiar route,
and nothing new
if you don't count
papers the wind
will sweep away
and in the alleys
orange lilies
that live a day.

Elders

The elect few
in Sunday best—
not saying much—
heard in the pew
the Word in Dutch,
bone and sinew
few could digest.

But every hymn
in common chords
if not manna
was bread to them,
a proof if man
could be certain
they were the Lord's.

Beside Myself

after Robert Walser

I'd wish this life
on no one else—
beside myself
who else could see
so much, could know
so much, and still
utter nothing,
almost nothing?

In Line

Who told me hold
this place in line?
How come it came
to seem like mine?

What will explain
the sense I get
of something that's
not happened yet?

At any rate
I grow older.
Am I the place
or the holder?

from POEMS AND PROBLEMS
(2007)

On the Way

There being
no way of
being there

—here being
by way of
being here—

there begins
a way of
not being

—beginning
being not
here nor there.

Details

Thinking I might
find the devil
in the details
I dropped my eyes
to street level
and found below
the curb's bevel
grass and pebbles,
glass and petals,
but I saw from
that angle no
fallen angel
in the gravel.

Pause

The likelihood
that the soul is,
that it endures
past these hours
of our selfhood,
preceding us
in utero
and exceeding
us engraved, is
nearly zero.
Still, the utter
unlikeliness
we should be gives
pause, a little.

Figures of Speech

So small the sets,
so stock the parts,
the *mise-en-scène*
seems like a masque
or mystery play,
and we the mimes,
all simile
and misery.

So much so, mind
itself shares in
the mimicry,
meek and smiling,
part King Herod,
part Mephisto,
all metaphor
and self-pity.

In Advance

Even given
where I come from
it is a shock
to find again
how far behind
I have become.

Taken aback,
I sprint ahead
to catch myself,
as if to reach
the very place
I never leave.

Reformers

No den mother,
Martin Luther
was less sullen
than John Calvin.

The Genevan
governed even
more grimly than
the Taliban.

Overheard

When Robert Frost
met Ezra Pound
they chose to talk
of Robinson.

And Paul Celan
met Heidegger
in part to speak
of Dickinson.

More than meeting
Oppen or Bronk
I would have liked
to listen in.

You Know the Way

Not having prepared for
the place prepared for me
I entered anyway
and found the bright raiments
and the precious patterns
just as had been promised.

Though not prodigal,
repentant, returning,
my welcome was as sweet
and my delight no less
for knowing, as I did,
I would not stay for long.

What We Learn

Going forward
the way is lit
by the same sword
cherubim burn
to prohibit
any return.

Their Marriage

She thinks of things
she wouldn't do
for anything
and things she'd do
anything for.

.

He thinks
what he
wouldn't
give for
things she
wouldn't
forgive.

Sight Unseen

to my wife

Love so blinds
I loved you
sight unseen,
but with years
the eyes clear
and I find
in hindsight
a love I'd
not foreseen.

Provision

Though my dim light
is little help
in the dark night
and adds nothing
to the bright day,

I love the slight
warmth it gives off
and hold it tight,
foreseeing chills
it might allay.

Ignoramus

If I knew where
poems issued from
I'd be excused
from writing more

and in despair
I would become
still more confused
what they are for.

So I ignore
the conundrum
and stay bemused,
if unaware.

Half-Sestina

ending with a line from Dickinson

I began thinking things
are to show what things are.
This consoled me somewhat.

Then I thought, you are what
things are for, maybe things
are to show what you are.

You may be what you are.
But because you are what
I hoped to find in things,

things are not what they are.

For Years I Dreamed

For years I dreamed
and thought my dreams
were dreams of loss,
dreams of years lost.

I thought I dreamed
the years were lost,
but thought's what lost
the years I dreamed.

Though nothing's lost
to years of dreams,
years are the dreams
of thought's losses.

Lakeside

It's hard now to recall
whatever I discerned
in the drift of it all.

As far as I'm concerned
whatever the waves call
has already returned.

Spectacle

In principle
my eyes are full.

In practice though
they overflow.

Thinking Back

What was new
made no sense.
What made sense
was the past.

Sense was made
in the past
and made sense
of the past.

The new was
past all sense.
What was new
was nonsense,

though nonsense
was not new.

When and Where

Where would here be
were I not here?
Does here need me
to be a here?
With me not here
would here float free?
Or would here be
here without me?

When I'm not here
will here hear me
calling, come here!
come stay with me?
Will here be near
without me here?
Or will I be
nowhere near here?

Suspended Sentence

Despite
the crimes
my dreams
disclose,
they grant
respite
if not
repose.

Delineation

Consider constellations,
how we want to ask of them
who first connected the dots
and found dippers or a face,

when the salient questions
are how the stars became dots
and who disconnected them,
spilt like dirt, in the first place.

In Essence

In extremis
it's the premise
that the I is
I finds amiss.

In excelsis
it's what else is
I dismisses
from existence.

The Drift

It's as if
all that's left
in the drift
is the draft
of some much
swifter flux

and as such
though it's felt
as a flow
of things lost
it's in fact
an influx.

The Stone

I sat on the step.
I stood by the shore.
I walked in the way.

What am I, I said,
and what is this voice,
and what are these limbs?

Then words answered me,
or I thought they did,
I thought I heard them.

They said, *vacancy.*
or else, v*agrancy,*
I couldn't be sure.

So I said myself,
I said to myself,
this: I am a stone.

I am a stone, I
am a stone, I am
a stone, I am...

But since then I brood.
Did I mean *a spark?*
or *a seed? a stick?*

Rebus

in homage to György Kurtág

I would
not be
but for
all which
are not.

Glimpse

Before my eyes
had seen what came
before my eyes
I saw what came
before eyes saw.

Looking

Though I toyed
with the thought
I was taught
not to look.

So with nose
in a book
I forsook
what I sought.

Which was all
that it took
to avoid
getting caught.

Now or Never

There have been moments,
hours here and there,
when for all intents
I was free and clear,

and God's absence rang
like a tongueless bell
and the angels sang
even as they fell.

Now though, these long months
of afternoon, when
what might have been once
has now never been.

For the Distance

He kept with her
for the distance
she kept from him.

She kept with him
for the distance
he kept her from.

The Past

The past still smolders
behind the fireline.
My boots caked with soot
kick at the charred boulders,
the seared stump and root,
eager to stamp out
what embers still shine.

Give and Take

I had taken
as a given
more is taken
than is given
and that givers
are on the take
and what I give
finds no takers.
But I give up,
I take it back,
you take the cake.
I can't take in
all you give in
our give and take.

How It Was

What I recall
is that a door
was where a wall
had been before.

Carmen LXXXV

Like Catullus,
both odious
and amorous.

Now That

Before
when you
were far
I thought
you were
not there.

Now that
I have
you near
I know
you are
not here.

All Told

Truth be told,
truth was told,
and the truth
left untold
took its toll,

but the truth
I heard told
I mistook,
thinking it
told for me.

Suddenly Wind

1

No Mohammed,
still the mountain
came down to me.
I mistook it
for an anthill.
Mount my summit!
it commanded.
I stepped on it.
Suddenly wind
tore at my throat
and my eyes froze.

2

Perhaps Sherpas
remember climbs.
All I recall
is that a voice
thundered at me:
Call me no more!
The rest is blank.
I'm back again.
The mound's unmoved,
except when ants
haul off a grain.

Once More

In the dry dunes
I learned to wring
my drink from stones.

And now beside
this brackish bay
I must again.

Eyesore

I scour for sights
to scour my sight,
but sights for sore eyes
make my eyes more sore.

Farewell

Little poem,
it won't be long
till I am gone.
What will become
of you then when
I'm not along?

Expect no friend
to comprehend
all you intend.
But you may find
one to remind
you what you found.

Do the Math

To measure my
desire for you
add one more to
all the days I
have gotten through.

Torch Song

Who so requires
my praise his fires
set even my
damp soul ablaze?

from A KNIFE IN MEN'S EYES
(2008)
and uncollected poems

for you beautiful ones my thought is not changeable
                    —*Sappho (trans. Anne Carson)*

A Knife in Men's Eyes

Her heels on the stones of Chişinău,
night never leaving the black branches.
Even at noon, night always in her hair.
Running a hand along the crumbling bricks
then later along the ancient path of her spine.
The spiral staircase inside the abbey,
damp with remembered noon heat.
Days of this. Wanting. She was
like a knife in men's eyes. A dark unnamed bird
slices the air. She returning into the blinding sun
after the struggle. Now later, the heart
thinks only of Pushkin in love,
in exile. The torn book left under the bed
in the hotel in Chişinău. Holds to this.
Holds to the sealed scroll in the archangel's hand.
As in the café, a taste in the heavy wine
held to the soil of the hills. Like blood.
Even knowing how roots rot soon after the vine,
between the black stones. Especially knowing this.

De rerum natura

Sonja turning away. Staring
at the rain glazing the dark window.
All the places on her he had touched.
Even then knowing they were memories
he touched, bruises eyes might leave behind,
the present pulsing through his fingers.
All day across the strasse the antennas
on the roof of the embassy transmitting
signals through the damp air, the wallpaper,
their bodies. As a boy riding out to see
the great hulks of barges in the narrow canal
not scraping either side. But keeping
his hand held back nonetheless.
Learning from the long lines in translation
how even lovers never penetrate.
Learning again each time. The infinitesimal
remove. Craving exactly that.

Cheating

Abba Marcarius who resolved to spend
five days in the presence of God.
Who entered his cell in the desert and stood
on a mat. Fighting with his thoughts.
Not coming down from heaven.
The demons becoming phantasms. Lions
who clawed at his legs. Black serpents
knotted, coital, collapsing. Flames
that consumed everything in the hut
but the soles of his feet. Until fire too fled him
and on the fifth day he understood
that were he to succeed, he would destroy
his understanding, himself, and would become
insanely arrogant. And so allowed again
the cares of the world to enter his heart.

Years Later

One's steady diet of regret. Feeding
on every window till the shattering of
proximity. Then the pension in Prague,
breaking in next door when we couldn't pay.
Beside the fence at the forest edge, in snow,
kneeling. Cucumbers and honey wine.
Trains as avid as we for distance.
Arriving at the farthest center and knowing
against all the enlightened had written
that spirit too could fail. Spirit most of all.
This was our high arcanum as
our bodies absorbed time's assault
and swayed without breaking. Her watching
the farmer hoist the sickle-shaped knife
and gut the stunned lamb. Neither sacrifice
nor redemption. Later the neighbors knocking
between our cries. Two weeks we feasted on
the bones of our hunger. Telling all this now,
muttering demented like Odysseus,
his shattered oar heaved to his shoulder.

Practice

Even across from me she was elsewhere, walking,
the sun rounding her shoulders, exposed,
her neck a tower as seen on a map. Paris,
Prague. Even across from me, others
saw her walking stone paths past them,
other windows glimmered at her passing.

This was to be expected. Sadly, though,
she too found herself unable to be where
she was. Her presence splintered the world
leaving multiple images of her without
original—like Helen, present variously
in Crete, in Tunis, the scented bed, walking.

It made saying goodbye no easier,
though it gave unending occasions for practice.

Figure and Ground

More than her body, he wanted the words
that applied to it. As though her body
would make real his own mind, such
aspiring. So that now the ins and outs
of each shape, the unspooling loops
and bends remind him of her alone.
Every contour he had traced repeats itself
before him. The shoreline bend, the sway
of the path, the sun's arc. The earth's
very curvature he knows because of her.
It occurs to him he had not seen her at all.
True, some memory had burned itself in.
But had it been the landscape all along?
Ascending the Raxalpe's massive uplift,
Webern's own dear summit. Hearing
her breathing. Evenings hearing how only
strictest austerities convey such lush craving.

Thinking they might heal
the very wounds they made him suffer.
Gladly. Now the curves, the ins and outs
of every shape, every object reminded him
of her. Every contour he had traced
repeats itself now before him. He cannot see
a building and not think of her in it, beside it.
The earth's very curvature he knows now

because of her. As though all that time
he had in fact been watching the sway
of the road, the shoreline bend, the sun's arc,
and not her. Some memory had burned itself in.
Ascending the Raxalpe's weightless mass,
Webern's own dear summit. Evenings hearing
how only strictest austerity can convey
such lush craving. Her black sleeves
above thin white wrists. Like writing.
The unspooling loops and twists. The brief
record of smoke from an extinguished wick.

The Glowing of Such Fire

Even dying—the dying more urgent
than everyday breakage and decay—
even near the end, with each breath
an engine of reluctance and will,
she sought to bruise him, to mark
his body, as though for future use.

So that now, years later, when memories
have swelled into clouds occluding
whatever sights he may still hope for,
now his body more than ever is alive
to her touch. The dark blossoms
on his arms, the tearing in his thigh,
the staggering crush of his ribs.

More than ever answering the pull.
Not the voice, but pulsing in her throat.
Not the glance, but the blinding disk
of her face. The black reed at the shore,
bent to the light's swell, or walking
the blond-grey stones to the Ægean,
at the water's serge edge: Sonja.

Their bodies had colluded like merchants,
leaving their anxious hearts to envy
such fierce exchange of bronze and gold.

In death no less than then, her
slow-rotting want exacting his,
reciprocal even in this weakening.
Insisting it too be hammered in.

Lauds

He cannot remember who he was. Rising,
he finds the man in the dim mirror. His eyes.
The man whose eyes had seen her narrow waist
bound in flame, her legs arch like ribs
of desert sand, her fingers, crimped petals
torn from their shaking stalk. The man knows
the lightning gash Saul of Tarsus thought
was the rending of the ancient world. He sinks
his face in the zinc basin. Hasn't he also heard
speaking so sudden it has yet to arrive
and suffered wounding so sovereign
it precedes even desire? Maybe so.

Later he will tell himself her name. By then
the vacant cave of morning will have softly shut.
He will think he has words to vindicate him,
smiling as he pockets the worthless ten lei coin.
He will be a man who must be forgiven.
For now though, he sits at his desk, not far
from where she'd be, and copies down again
the lie from Cowley, *"Her Body is my Soul."*

Crete

Even after a year, after the fables they told themselves,
ones about the missed ferry, the torn raincoat, the stolen pears—
claiming the blunders and hazards of love as the truest tokens
of divine election—he could not account for her body. Mornings,
there beside him, taut and slack as a length of rope. As though
Icarus had found this bed instead of the cold plaited sea
to break his fall, the white sheets lapping the still-warm flesh
  in unction.

Her shoulder blades alone were an insult to his understanding.
Plato called them stubs of wings, but better was Pheidias, who
  saw more
and knew to clasp Athena's golden ægis over their exposed splendor.
Or Rodin. Who was simply driven mad by them.
Granted, he could not unravel this. Still his eyes wept with avarice,
willing him to look. Looking while he started the coffee, laughing
at his ignorance, buttering the stale bread, looking. Hungry to know.

A Course in Miracles

He distrusted his own body; it was hers
whose wisdom he craved. *As the hart panteth
after the water brooks*, he thought. He hungered
for her body's voice, how in its syllables he heard
what he was allowed of the greater mysteries.
Touching her now, asleep, her hair a shawl
lowered over an ancient scroll, he contemplated
the non-existence of the body. These shoulders,
he muttered, do not mean anything. This hollow
as if cut by a river along her spine, her thighs
like twin saplings—like words, they do not exist.
He looked over toward the rain-streaked window,
summer daylight fading like calfskin in candlelight:
this was the body's wisdom, that it is not real.
This knowledge was the fiery corona he saw now
fringing her long contours. Were all such initiations,
he wondered, so perfectly ordinary? so sadly enough?
She stirred and seemed to sigh. He turned and slept.

Near the Terminal

ending with a reference
to Edith Wharton

Before he saw the world righting itself
as she stepped onto the platform, before
his vertigo stilled as he gripped her bags,
before they joined the crowd over the station bridge,
the lurching train's final vehement shriek
had settled a petulance in him. So that now,
amid the urgencies, he could contemplate
at will a cursive twist of hair and how
the mirror near the grey window seemed lit
by the sourceless light of dreams, the light
eyes embezzle from the day, the sheen
from before God made the sun and moon.
He watched the negligent eddying of the world
and turned back toward her face, cast for him now
in half-relief, so close that sight was smell.
On the pillow her empty fist was a prayer.
And in the oblivion, only echoes—a gasp,
a locomotive keening, and at midnight black
rain pelting the roof of the station.

Campsite

He sees his nothingness, who most does love desire.
—Christopher Witt

He turned and saw her in the absences between the trees.
The dark hollows between the trunks taunted him, or seemed to.
Like Kelpius near the Wissahickon, he thought: the Woman
in the Wilderness, ever receding as the heavens rattled
in flame, though when he looked the early stars defeated him,
puzzlingly indifferent to his wish to find her torso there.

It was then he heard the ceaseless sobbing of his heart.
And had the bleat of children not distracted him, the sound
he nearly made would have turned the moon to blood.
Strange comfort nonetheless to know again such prayer
persisted in his tired skin, like a coiled rustling in the leaves
on the forest floor the dampness had carpeted for her.

His borrowed camper was no grotto, his indigence
no ravished poverty of soul. The agonies he underwent
were cramps and mediocrities. And yet there hammered
in the tongueless bell his skull had forged a silence
with a name, a ringing vacancy answering his,
like thunder on a mountain, like cataracts on quartz.

First Principles

She promised what he wanted, promised
not just light but light unfading. And for all
he knew of guile and sorrow and flesh, he knew
he was capable of that. Capable, if not of the eternal,
of its eternally willed counterpart. Capable, that is,
if she was, if she truly promised this: he required
only her complicity. Afford me one edge, he thought,
one arc to activate with devotion bordering
on sacrilege, breaching that border, and I
shall not fail to bring desire, regardless of
what desire may bring. He consoled himself
with this hubris and looked up from his work.
It's true, he vowed. Just this, and some money.

Talisman

The room was square, with a window to the left
through which a dry wind would reach in
and grab his shoulder; but otherwise he wrote
unmolested. The window with its grid of wires
and graffitied walls depicted a transcendence
imbricated and abstract enough for him to ignore.
His concerns were elsewhere. So when he heard
her steps like a jeweler's hammer in the hall
he would stand—the early evening light brushing
his back like someone's hand stroking farewell—
to leave with her, but not before dropping a stone
on a sheaf of papers, where in his absence it lay,
flat as a nailhead, shadows sifting around it,
as if to warn any who might come not to read
his work unless they too knew what pleasures live
in the thoughts of a troubled man, unless they too
had demolished themselves by their own strength
and found in sadness a noble destitution like joy,
glad like him to be such a one thus riven through.

Quatrain from a Dream

From where he stood the window was hid
but a rectangle of light hung reflected
in the fearsome rain like a sheet put out
after a first night of love. Or so he thought.

Last Sayings

All around him were the things he could not heal.
Jesus among the microbes, he thought. The twinge
in his side was nothing. But on his desk books
bloomed like sores along the leprous body of the world.
Or, better, like the blue lesions on the cheap print
of the Grünewald altar tacked beside his door.
And he had thought to cure these! Well, not today.
Today he could think only of the ink-stain dullness
of his past, the boy in whose scuffed shoes he had walked
beneath a Michigan sky helmeted over with grief,
something like grief. A vinegar taste under his tongue.
And in his dreams, horizonless convulsions of waves.
How had desire ever broken in? A dark light glinting
off the crockery? A high thin song sounding in
the dogged drone of frozen pipes and fearful men?
He almost laughed: had a knife pierced his side?
How had the clotted flesh ever come to such aspiring?
He might never know, or only after transformations
so complete he would be left nursing far other wounds,
others' wounds. For now, his knowledge was confined
to a sharp ringing in his temples and a trembling,
like a fast freezing creek, along his outstretched arm.

In defeat to feel at last the form desire failed to take.

As though failure were the purest form desire knew.

His Discontent

What he wanted was to live, at least that's how he put it.
He was a man who thought that life was kept from him.
Sometimes his lungs would fill with almost viscid rage
as if he were himself the imbecile brother he never knew.
Other times his skin hung on him like a desiccated caul
and sorrow draped about him like a borrowed suit.
So it came as a surprise one day to find he was immortal.
He woke, saying of himself what is true of the mind:
I am immortal, he said, and knew that it was so.
I cannot be destroyed, he said, and knew his strength.

He rose and walked about the holy city of Baltimore
and said of the drab trees choking in the gauzy dust
and of the squat brown benches and the listing steeples:
you are eternal. Because I see you it is so.
He found the ageless now where he had always sought it.
It shopped the Rite Aid pharmacy, it hid in the weeds
that rimmed the blistered parking lot, it blazoned the sky.
Perhaps this should not have been a surprise. After all,
certain books had been opened even to him, and women
had unsealed to him the blinding swiftness of their beauty.

Maybe the surprise was not his immortality at all
but that one could know even this and still not have lived.

Sonja Standing

Sonja standing in the narrow room. Always this.
The ceiling high above her. The pattern
elaborating along its edges interrupted
by the nearest wall. His hand against that wall.
Evidence, then, of more expansive pasts,
grander rooms, disclosing space to eyes
keener than his, able to purchase fuller scenes,
shadows even richer, and still more refulgent flames.
But always for him her standing there,
the ceiling vaulted over, the bed's edge
a measure to help him know precisely this,
the endless shoreline of her thighs,
the carved altar of her back, its proportions
matching some ordained, forgotten ratio.
Twisting to adjust a line, bending to reach down,
she became the very principle of his sight.
And if his way was one of contraction—
restricting knowledge to things seen, delimiting
rooms to narrow walls, a high ceiling,
a bed, a tessellated floor, a broken pattern
in the antique molding—there was always this:
the exacting curve of her hair, the balancing length
of one arm as the other absent-mindedly bends
to her intent, retrieving a passing want. Always this.

Head of Orpheus

The ordered waves sound over me like strings—
I, the plectrum. Purple kelp garlands my brow.
My hair bobs like a mass of drifting wood.
My eyes are two flat stones: too like sunlight
glistening off the rippling crests to sink.
Brine sloshes through my mouth and gladdens me.
At last I've found my element, between the sky's
grey matter and the hollow body of the sea.

The song we give the earth is memory,
death the tide that buoys the spindrift words.
The chambers of my mind recall her now,
ripped from sentience faster than forgetting.
The blackness of her hair flamed after her
against the lesser darkness of the night.
My head was severed from my body then,
and I became a man without regret.

Yet remorse perfects my windburned lips
into a dolphin smile. The shrieks of seagulls wash
her darting footsteps from my conch-shell ears.
I stare for days at jostling disks of cloud,
imagining a distant, narrow beach,
a blinding neck of sand, red grass, the trees
like stringless dulcimers, a figure watching
as my skull navigates the riptide swells.

Oedipus

We don't like to think about what he did,
though it's all we actually remember.
Everyone forgets what happened after,
which is how he wanted it—making a bid
for the longevity of a human affection,
chancing on shame as having better odds
even than love, especially even than love.

Wandering the wastes, begging scraps,
preferring disdain to pity, needing only
the loyalty of his daughters, he strove
to make it last, to be a monument, himself
the stone set before the sepulchers
of men's eyes. No man had done more.

And yet the winds whirling in his eye-pits
became a kind of light, and in spite of
all he'd done he found that he could see.
Butterflies leaped the fractured rocks like tigers.
Milkweed pods bit down on tufts of fur.
In the distance, the great holdings of the city.

And if these were merely apparitions of
his soul's imaginary sight, they restored to him
a tableau even he could not destroy.

The Campaign

I entered the ruined city despite myself. In places
the cries were deafening. Flames flooded from windows.
Charred tires, collapsed tenements blocked my way.
A man carrying a paper bag stormed past me bleating,
"This never could have happened!" Another man
offered me his burnt-out pickup, smiling madly. At last
I found my father's house and in it the careful wreckage
of his unlived life. "Father," I said, "let me carry you."
He bent forward in his chair and hung his arms
around my neck. He was as heavy as a stove.
On our way out he flung up an arm and grabbed the cross
that had long dangled over the threshold. My wife
and children followed us. The devastation we passed
was unspeakable. At last we collapsed in a green field
beneath a sprawling sycamore, its strewn fruit bristling
at our feet. My father rubbed the soot from his face
with the back of his wilted hand. "Son, when we return
I will speak of you favorably to my friends who still remain."

Leaving Baltimore

My friend Joe Harrison probably put it best
when he said, "Baltimore's a good place to leave."

Billie Holiday left when she was thirteen.
Frank Zappa at eleven. Upton Sinclair
at ten. Frank O'Hara left at eighteen months.
Did any one of them ever make it back?
Adrienne Rich left. Philip Glass left, leaving
behind his father's radio repair shop.
Tupac Shakur attended the Baltimore
School for the Arts, then left. And needless to say
Gertrude Stein departed. "Once upon a time,"
she proclaimed, "Baltimore was necessary."

"The best image to sum up the unconscious
is Baltimore in the early morning" was
Jacques Lacan's observation before he left.
Henry James visited, then left, this "cheerful
little city of the dead." Francis Scott Key
was once famously detained near Baltimore,
and he later returned to die in his sleep.
Edgar Allan Poe wasn't able to leave,
and now tourists come to drink toasts at his tomb.
Ogden Nash fell in love with Frances Leonard,
a Baltimore belle, and he died here as well.
Lizette Woodworth Reese was born here and remained.
Is that why so few ever read *The York Road*?

Zelda Fitzgerald stayed at the Phipps Clinic
and Sheppard Pratt before leaving for Asheville.
Sidney Lanier left, but not before he wrote
the line, "The worker must pass to his work in
the terrible town." Louis Zukofsky worked
at an engineering firm, but he soon left.
My teacher Hugh Kenner left. Richard Sober
left, though I still do have a painting of his.
And I wonder where Laurens Dorsey could be.
Laurens was a friend. He warned me he would leave.

Emerson left after seeing a pulpit
that could rotate like a railyard turntable.
Nearing death, Whitman refused to take a train
to consult Dr. Osler at Johns Hopkins,
though he did once propose to Peter Doyle
that they live together "in some quiet place"
in Baltimore. Countee Cullen was born in
Baltimore, or maybe it was Louisville.
Once he claimed he was born in New York City,
but he may have meant that metaphorically.
Nina Simone recorded a song about
Baltimore, as did Bob Dylan and Carmen
McRae, which only shows you don't need to live
here to leave. Bruce Springsteen sang about a guy
who left his "wife and kids in Baltimore, Jack."

Thinking all this makes me want to do the same:
at least maybe I'd get a poem out of it
or be like Emily Dickinson, who asked
"if there *was* any moon in Baltimore," or
A.R. Ammons. "Poetry in Baltimore,"
he said, "for some reason seems incongruous."

Charles & 25th Streets

Where the bookstore used to be
a pharmacy is going up.

I have read too many books.
What is the medicine for that?

from TRIADS
(2011)

I console myself a little by turning the self at each moment into words and reading them.

—*Ishikawa Takuboku*

The brown sky
above the four-story apartment building
looks like a blanket.

Looking up
I see the curtains are tied back
in the top-floor apartment.

The painting I wanted to buy of an underpass
which I thought would show my peculiar sensibility—
I often think of it.

It's nice to see
three people coming out of weekday mass.
I like not going there.

I write to sound striking
when translated
into Dutch.

Twice she came to me in a dream.
First she dismissed me,
then she allowed me to stay.

The noise from the airport bar—
I walk past
with my children.

I relaxed when I saw
the small hollow under the snow-covered bush—
there's shelter everywhere.

Fear, then delight,
finding my enemy
shopping at the same store I was.

I was happy all day
after getting to be angry
for a good reason.

I remember the long trenches I dug with my heel
on rainy days
at recess.

I still remember the silver locket
of the neighbor girl
who played at hypnotizing me.

The teacher we ridiculed in middle-school—
I cheated on a test
in order to dislike her more.

The dog tugged on the leash
all the way out
and all the way back.

Driving by a well-lit coffee shop
my desire flares—
and I don't even like coffee!

While I fretted over putting my toe in
the water rose
above my head.

The smell of perfume
beneath the streetlight
wrecked any chance I had of sobriety that night.

The roots tear underneath,
but the shadows of the branches
caress the ground like a lover.

Today I sent my daughters to school
without their coats.
I wore mine, though.

Now I know it was your absence
that made the past incomplete,
and thus worth remembering.

I stood in the aisle a long time
looking for a Valentine card
that didn't say too much.

The ship I hoped would rescue me
is carefully sealed
in the same bottle I put the message in.

Like a difficult child,
I finally calm down
when I hear something truly serious.

If only I always felt about others
the way I feel about them
when I'm drunk.

I've put away
childish things,
but they are within easy reach.

I am a tree
when there is no wind,
trying to flap its branches.

The chimney smoke
twitched in the wind
like the tail of a menacing squirrel.

Not everything is beautiful, I thought,
but the beautiful things
are very, very beautiful.

Immense, spontaneous gratitude
when in the presence
of human competence.

Again and again I return
to the scene of a crime
I will someday have the courage to commit.

The first hot day,
and the air conditioners are popping out of windows
like failed suicides.

I may not dwell in possibility
but it felt good just now
to see a FOR RENT sign.

Between the new cinderblock wall
and the fresh sidewalk
someone has planted an oak tree.

I am satisfied only when
my present seems like a past
I enter through someone else's memory.

I like the songs that end
by trying to recall
the silence they began by interrupting.

I worship a volcano god
and wear the teeth of its victims
as charms against its foe, the sea.

A mother chasing after a chicken
but leaving her boy behind—
how later the boy will feel about chickens.

It's still summer, of course,
but that one cloud
looks like the rake hanging in the rafters.

Like someone done with work,
and done with dinner,
but unable to find the remote.

Yes, I have untied the knot
my mind was in for so long,
but there is still a kink in the rope.

I learned to love the world
when I learned the world could not be loved
all at once.

These poems began in an effort to understand and love poetry more. Although publication was intrinsic to the art I wanted to learn, it was far down the agenda. The advice of Epicurus was what I needed: λάθε βιώσας, live obscurely. That way there might be hope for the necessary time and quiet.

But order was needed, too. Finishing poems before putting them aside would be important, and I couldn't honestly expect anyone to help with this. So along with poetry, I had a chance to learn more about printing and book-making, crafts whose glamor came from my earliest memories of my father's printing business. I made each of the books from which the poems in this volume come using different methods: setting lead type by hand, printing on letterpress, binding the books myself, using composition software, printing digitally. While learning more about poetry, I could learn more about books, too. The limited runs were as much the result of my resources and skill as the consequence of my restricted poetic. That eleven books came about (I've kept out of this volume any selections from *Scattered Remains*, a book of aphorisms) is a measure of the corresponding drive.

I took some justification for my procedure from Charles Reznikoff, who pursued a similar method: "since I did not hope for a publisher / to print my verse soon at his own risk," Reznikoff recalled, "why, I thought, I should print privately…"

There was little notice to be had that way, I knew,
among the crowd of new books;

but, besides the stimulation to write and revise,
I would clear my head and heart
for new work. Yes, the work was the thing.

That the work was the thing was one lesson I had to learn.

Like publishing and writing, and meaning and meter, understanding and love are only uneasily made compatible. Maybe love arises in the gaps, even the absence, of understanding, just as pleasure may emerge as the absence of pain. Epicurus noted that if we weren't so fearful we would have no need for knowledge. He also noted that our greatest pleasures come from the things that used to make us most afraid. To write poetry, then, is to enjoy something with which you will perpetually be least content. Doing so clears the way for new work and new life.

ACKNOWLEDGMENTS

Thanks to the editors of the journals in which some of these poems previously appeared: *City Paper*, *Poet Lore*, *Sewanee Theological Review*, *The Shattered Wig Review*, and *32 Poems*.

Thanks also to the Maryland State Arts Council for Individual Artist Awards in 2009 and 2011.